CATERPILLAR TEN

Including 7C Fifteen and High Fifteen

PHOTO ARCHIVE

Bob LaVoie

Iconografix
Photo Archive Series

Iconografix
PO Box 446
Hudson, Wisconsin 54016 USA

Iconografix books are offered at a discount when sold in quantity for promotional use. Businesses or organizations seeking details should write to the Marketing Department, Iconografix, at the above address.

Library of Congress Card Number: 99-76052

ISBN 1-58388-011-9

00 01 02 03 04 05 06 5 4 3 2 1

Printed in the United States of America

Cover and book design by Shawn Glidden

Copy editing by Dylan Frautschi

Iconografix Inc. exists to preserve history through the publication of notable photographic archives and the list of titles under the Iconografix imprint is constantly growing. Transportation enthusiasts should be on the Iconografix mailing list and are invited to write and ask for a catalog, free of charge.

Authors and editors in the field of transportation history are invited to contact the Editorial Department at Iconografix, Inc., PO Box 446, Hudson, WI 54016. We require a minimum of 120 photographs per subject. We prefer subjects narrow in focus, e.g., a specific model, railroad, or racing venue. Photographs must be of high quality, suited to large format reproduction.

PREFACE

The histories of machines and mechanical gadgets are contained in the books, journals, correspondence, and personal papers stored in libraries and archives throughout the world. Written in tens of languages, covering thousands of subjects, the stories are recorded in millions of words.

Words are powerful. Yet, the impact of a single image, a photograph or an illustration, often relates more than dozens of pages of text. Fortunately, many of the libraries and archives that house the words also preserve the images.

In the *Photo Archive Series,* Iconografix reproduces photographs and illustrations selected from public and private collections. The images are chosen to tell a story—to capture the character of their subject. Reproduced as found, they are accompanied by the captions made available by the archive.

The Iconografix *Photo Archive Series* is dedicated to young and old alike, the enthusiast, the collector and anyone who, like us, is fascinated by "things" mechanical.

ACKNOWLEDGMENTS

The photographs, captions, and related information included in this book were made available by the Caterpillar Inc. Corporate Archives.

Table of Contents

Ten at the Massachusetts State Fair display for M.B. Tyler Company. This tractor appears to be painted white for its special appearance.

INTRODUCTION

In late 1928, Caterpillar Tractor Company unveiled the model Ten tractor. Weighing in at 4,500 pounds, it was the smallest tractor to be made by the company, and at the time, filled a gap in the small crawler-tractor marketplace. Unfortunately, the model Ten was born with design problems, and from early on, its future was dim. When the tractor was discontinued in 1932, only 4,929 units had been made. This was a fairly sizable number of tractors when compared to other Caterpillar models marketed in the era, but not as impressive as some other models made by other manufacturers.

The tractor was available in standard or narrow gauge at 37 inches, wide gauge at 44 inches, an orchard or tail seat version in both gauges, and a high-clearance model. The standard high-clearance Ten was a 44-inch gauge. This is the same gauge width as the wide gauge low Ten. It is unclear how many versions were made. All variations of the model Ten carried the "PT" serial number prefix, and no additional designations were issued to the special units.

In 1932, Caterpillar introduced two "new" redesigned machines. The modifications made to the tractors were all lessons learned from the model Ten and PV Fifteen. The new tractors, known as the 8C Twenty, or small Twenty, and the 7C Fifteen, or small Fifteen, incorporated new technology that was to be used for several years.

When the model Ten was discontinued, a small tractor was needed to replace it in the product line. Apparently, owing to the fact that the Ten was producing 15 horsepower, it was decided to correct the Ten's problems, but keep the basic design.

When the 7C Fifteen was introduced in 1932, it looked like a totally different tractor. The new tractor sported the bright Highway Yellow color with bold, black decals. The old over-the-engine location for the gas tank was moved ahead of the operator and served as the firewall. This allowed the exhaust outlet to pass through a hole in the hood, rather than around the hood, since the gas tank was now moved. The simple modification corrected the Ten's old problem of heat transferring to the gas tank. Also, the delicate cast-iron dash of the model Ten was eliminated.

The high-clearance model is simply a small Fifteen lifted to a total clearance of 24 inches with a high Ten undercarriage. It is unknown if any small Fifteens were lifted by using a kit from a high Ten by anybody other than the factory. If you discover a high Fifteen with a 7C prefix, you probably have found a conversion. This was the last attempt at a high-clearance crawler. It was rumored that a photo of a high-clearance Fifteen or Ten was seen hanging on the wall of a chief executive's office in the 1930s to remind him of how much money was lost with the high-clearance endeavor.

Why so few of this innovative little tractor were produced is a mystery. The engineering built into it paved the way for many other models to follow. Using much of this technology, the model Twenty-Two was a huge success in the small tractor market.

Caterpillar 4C series mower ready to be fitted to a standard Ten tractor. 175 4C series mowers were produced with other mowers being made by the Detroit Mower Company and the Rawls Manufacturing Company.

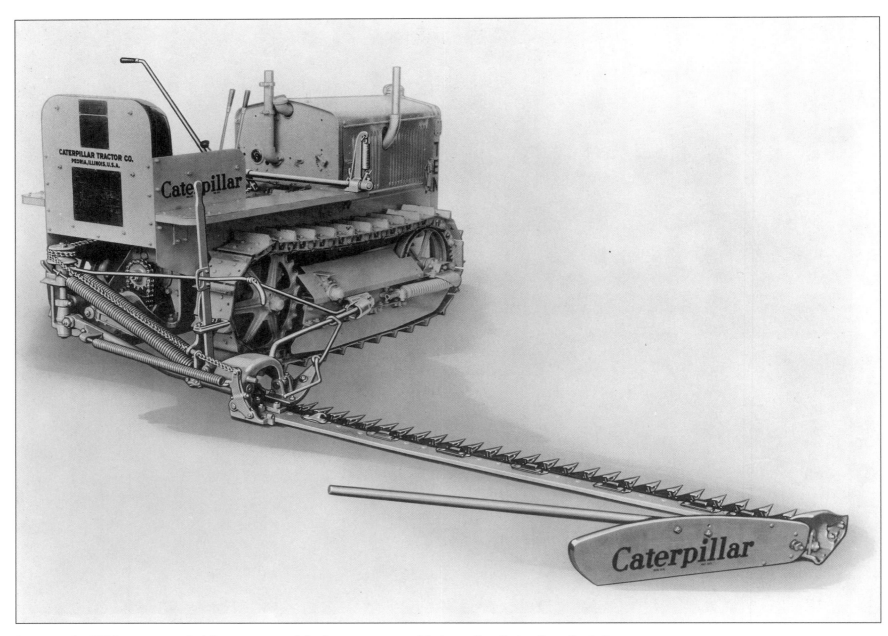

Ten with PTO powered 4C series sickle bar mower. Notice the late decal style.

Ten pulling a combine in a Montana field.

Factory photo of a narrow gauge Ten.

Ten serial number PT3306 in a factory photo showing belt pulley drive unit. Also notice the decal style and placement. The rear seat decal seems to be white or gray with a darker, possibly red border.

Winter model Ten equipped with cab, lights, skeleton tracks, tow hook, and radiator curtain. Notice the decal placement on the hood and cab doors.

Ten equipped with lights and snowplow removing snow from city sidewalks.

Ten pulling Ann Arbor baler in a Michigan field in 1930.

Mother and daughter team operates a Ten in a 1929 photo. Notice the absence of decals and highlight paint on the model and radiator designation.

October 1930 at the Peoria Country Club, a Ten spreads fertilizer. This machine also seems to be lacking decals and lettering paint.

Ten working in a Kansas field in June 1930.

Standard Ten pulling a 14-foot disc in a California field.

Ten pulling a corn picker through a soft Minnesota field, 1929.

Ten pulling a 3-disc plow in second gear.

Fred Cyphers uses his Ten in December 1931 to spread manure on a snowy field.

Ten owned by the University of Oxford on loan to the Norfolk Agriculture Station in Sprowston, Norwich, England. It is seen with a Babcock model "C" cultivator working in sugar beets.

A Ten equipped with a LaPlant Choate blade clears snow from the Canadian National Railway shop yard.

Ten mowing the fairways at the New Orleans Country Club in March 1931.

At the Transport Air Terminal in Winslow, Arizona, a Ten is used to pull Transcontinental Air Transport planes into position.

Frank Jarvis of Rowena, Oregon uses his wide gauge Ten to skid logs in April 1931. Notice this wide gauge tractor is equipped with standard width track pads.

Pulling the welder sled on the 12 inch Sinclair Pipeline from Gladwater to Mesia, Texas, a Ten works in June 1931.

Ten with Ann Arbor baler in June 1929.

Peninsula Paving Company of San Mateo, California uses a Ten and a Fresno Scraper to grade a street in May 1929.

Ten with Dempster push rake carrying soybean hay to a baler in October 1929.

E.T. Smith of Hartsville, Ohio uses his wide gauge Ten to pull a disc and Dunham packer in October 1931.

Wide gauge Ten with swamp pads hauls onions from a field near Toledo, Ohio in March 1930.

34

Joe Bucknam of Sedalia, Ohio uses his Ten with LaPlant Choate snowplow to haul Christmas trees to market in December 1932.

Ten pulling a hay baler in June 1930.

Tractor Trader provides this photo of a Ten with Babcock model "C" cultivator working at the Norfolk Agricultural Station at Sprowston, Norwich, England in July 1932.

Ten pulling model 38 Holt combine with 12-foot header combining oats. The tractor pulls the combine in high gear, except when turning.

Operator of the Ten waves to Charles Lindbergh as Charles begins his first transcontinental flight from Los Angeles in 1929. Also pictured is Amelia Earhart. Notice the T.A.T. decal applied to the dirt shield, designating Transcontinental Air Transport.

Ten with Rawls mower cutting weeds along the railroad near Metamora, Illinois.

Ten with S-gang mower, mowing fairways at the Peoria Country Club in October 1930. Notice the rear belt pulley drive attachment.

Owner C.S. Fogwell of Maricopa County, Arizona uses her Ten with subsoiler to tend to her grapefruit orchard. This machine is equipped with full enclosure citrus fenders. Also notice the undulating decal located on the seat back, normally found only on the seat sides.

S.D. Gillespie of Lookout, Wyoming uses his Ten and 7-foot 4C series Caterpillar mower to cut wild grass in August 1932.

Ten, working in second gear, pulls a 2-bottom Rock Island plow through a heavy growth of weeds and corn stalks in July 1930.

Miller Farm and Greenhouse use their Ten to pull a spring tooth harrow through a Toledo greenhouse in September 1930.

The city of Elmhurst, Illinois uses its Ten with LaPlant Choate plow to clear sidewalks after a February 1933 storm.

Ten works skidding logs near Mission, San Jose, California in June 1929.

Factory photo of standard gauge Ten, taken in April 1930. Notice the absence of a pre-cleaner on the air intake stack and also the decal locations.

Orchard model or tail seat Ten in a company photo. Notice the decal locations on the hood and firewall due to the different configuration of the seat and fenders.

Side view of the tail seat Ten showing a better view of decal locations and control levers.

50

Rear view of tail seat Ten showing operator's area and mounting of control levers. Notice the normally foot operated clutch is now hand operated with the lever to the far left.

Right rear view of tail seat Ten, showing the side view of the fenders. These fenders differ from the Bishop style citrus fenders, which are fully enclosed.

Standard gauge Ten equipped with F.S. Bishop citrus fenders installed by Freeland Tractor Company for orchard work.

April 1930 factory photo of standard gauge Ten.

Factory photo of standard Ten equipped with front guard or push plate in November 1929.

Ten equipped with open canopy. Notice the locations of the decals. The seat side decal has been moved to the engine hood so the view would not be obstructed.

Ten wide gauge "Swamp Special" in a 1929 company photo.

Ten equipped with Willamette single drum hoist. Notice the raised conventional seat back and auxiliary seat for operating the winch.

Factory photo taken in July 1930, showing the new screened engine side curtains on a standard gauge tractor. These apparently replaced the old louvered style side curtains.

Winter model Ten equipped with cab, lights, tow hook, skeleton ice tracks, and radiator curtain. Notice the decal locations on the machine equipped with a cab.

Factory photo of Ten with cab equipped with a LaPlant Choate sidewalk plow.

Rear view of Ten equipped with cab and skeleton tracks for winter work, clearly showing the decal placement on the rear of the cab.

Ten with standard tracks equipped with street plates for use on hard surfaces or paved roads.

Ten equipped with Rawls PTO operated mower. The sickle can be raised or lowered to clear obstructions and is equipped with a shear pin in case an object is hit.

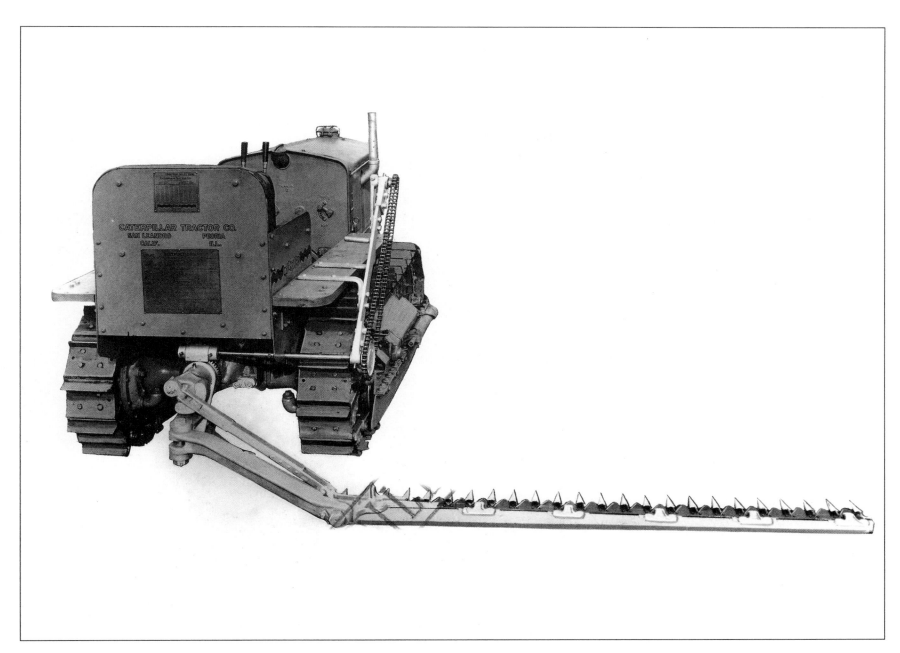

Factory photo of standard Ten with PTO driven 7-foot mower.

Ten owned by the city of St. Louis, Missouri, fitted with a Detroit mower, cutting in the Chain of Rocks Park.

Winter equipped Ten pulls a sleigh of lumber to the storage yard at a Wisconsin mill.

Ten equipped with broom sweeps snow from the streets in Outremount, Quebec, Canada, in March 1931.

Pennsylvania State College uses its Ten equipped with rotary broom to clear snow in May 1932.

The Mutual Chemical Company of Baltimore, Maryland, uses its push plate equipped Ten to push a 70,000-pound car of chrome ore into the factory.

Factory photo of engine and rear end of the Ten for a company sales brochure. Notice the Eisemann GV4 magneto.

Standard Ten equipped with Dempster push rake.

Factory photo taken in December 1931 of a wide gauge Ten with standard width tracks. Notice the late decal style font on the seat side shown.

Bayville Farms of Lynnhaven, Virginia, use their Ten with stationary belt drive to operate a silage cutter and silo filler in October 1929.

Dune Lakes Ltd. of Santa Barbara, California uses a wide gauge Ten to pull an aquatic mower from one lake to another on the wild game refuge in January 1932.

A standard gauge Ten moves logging high wheelers to a storage area at a factory yard in November 1928.

Forrest Home Cemetery of Milwaukee, Wisconsin uses its model Ten with rubber track pads to clean up autumn leaves. Notice the late decal style on the seat side and also the LaPlant Choate blade arms and lift to accommodate a snowplow.

Ten tractors, owned by H.E. Drake of Visalia, California, working with rotary scrapers in a heavy lime deposit, November 1931.

Baltimore Street Department using a push blade equipped Ten to clean leaves from city streets in 1930.

Ten with mower working in third gear along a Sheboygan, Wisconsin roadway in 1930. Notice how the operator tows his car conveniently behind him during his day's work.

H.C. Crockett of Old Mission, Michigan drives his Ten like a team of horses through his cherry orchard. Pulling on both reins will release both steering clutches, thus stopping the tractor.

Coos Bay Lumber Company of Bay Point, California uses its push plate equipped Ten to move thirty cars of lumber weighing 105 tons in May 1929.

Standard Ten with rubber track pads, pulling a #1 9B series Terracer through a Peoria subdivision, grading a road in 1930.

Ten equipped with lights, cab, and a LaPlant Choate hand lift blade working at a Chicago landfill in December 1929.

High-clearance Ten equipped with push plate and lights. Notice the large spot type light and the newer style decal font on the seat side.

Harvey Firestone of Columbiana, Ohio bought the first high Ten in the state. Here he uses it to disc near his home in April 1931. Notice the absence of sprocket guards on this early high Ten.

Stockton Brothers of Sheridan, Wyoming use their high Ten and Babcock weed cultivator in a corn field in 1931.

High Ten working near Erie, Pennsylvania, pulling a 2-18 Oliver plow in second gear, cutting a 10-inch furrow. April 5 1931.

U.S. Siegrist uses his high Ten and Aurora plow near Denver, Colorado in March 1932.

High Ten and Dempster 3-row Lister Cultivator working in May 1932 on the Clappey Farm at Albany, Georgia.

High Ten with low set, free-swinging draw bar, pulling a 5-foot chisel in second gear. February 1931.

Working near Aurora, Colorado in December 1931, a high Ten pulls a John Deere 2-bottom plow 10 inches deep in low moisture soil.

High Ten and 9B series #1 Terracer work near Atchison, Kansas in 1931 on a drainage ditch project.

Final cultivation of corn and beans on the Clappey Farm at Albany, Georgia. The high Ten is equipped with a Rock Island model RIC cultivator. June 1932.

High Ten with 3-row mechanical lift cultivator working near San Leandro, California in October 1931. Notice the absence of decals, dirt guards, and sprocket shields on this high Ten.

High Ten with special tree digger attachment, harvesting 20-foot poplar trees at the Stark Nursery in Missouri. June 1931.

Mr. C. Koward of Aurora, Colorado uses his high Ten and John Deere 3-row weeder on his 700 acre farming operation in July 1931.

Owner A.W. Feeser of Silver Run, Maryland uses his high Ten, roller, and harrow readying ground for his pea and cabbage crop. June 1931. Notice the absence of rear sprocket guards on this early high Ten.

St. Procopius College at Lisle, Illinois uses its high Ten and 2-14 plow for many tasks around the orchard in November 1932.

F.C. Stahelin Nursery of Bridgeman, Michigan uses its high Ten and Babcock cultivator in June 1931.

Factory photo with seat removed showing location and mounting of the rear mechanical lift group. This unit also included a PTO shaft, which is located under the rear cover. This unit utilized a dog clutch and rockshaft to raise and lower tillage and ground engaging tools. It was activated by the taller lever to the right of the steering levers and engaged by the standard PTO control lever.

High Ten equipped with 3-row Killefer cultivator. This machine is being used by the Stockton Bros. of Sheridan, Oregon 1931.

High Ten with Babcock cultivator working on Bain Smith's farm at Lyford, Texas in March 1931.

High Ten with late style decal font working in an Alabama field. This decal appears to be darker in color with a lighter border, possibly red with a gray or silver border. This tractor is also equipped with the rear mechanical lift unit.

Front view of prototype high Ten serial number PT2572 showing ground clearance. 1929.

Side view of prototype high Ten absent of rear sprocket shields as shown in a 1929 company photo.

Rear of high Ten prototype showing operator height and visibility.

PT2572 prototype high Ten with low draw bar installed.

Rear view of high Ten showing ground clearance with low draw bar removed.

7C small Fifteen wide gauge owned by Jack Campbell of Hillside, Colorado is working to clear a path to a 300 head feedlot after a 1933 storm.

7C Fifteen at work at the Cassela Brothers apple orchard at Swedesboro, New Jersey in June 1932.

Fifteen 7C series equipped with Moro 18-inch hand lift plow on July 4, 1933.

Rear of Fifteen 7C series equipped with Moro 2-way plow.

Standard gauge 7C Fifteen at work for Cassela Brothers of Swedesboro, New Jersey.

Standard gauge 7C Fifteen equipped with Bishop citrus fenders. Machine is driven by actor Clark Gable.

Fan Dancer Sally Rand's mother, Mrs. Ernest Kisling inspects her 7C Fifteen orchard model that was given to her by Sally for Christmas in 1932. It was used in their 1900 tree grove near Glendora, California. This view gives a good look at the new manifold design and horizontally louvered side curtains.

Rear upper view of 7C Fifteen in a company photo showing decal placement.

7C Fifteen cultivating blackberries at the Purdue University Horticultural farm at Lafayette, Indiana.

7C Fifteen and Moro 2-way hand lift plow demonstrated at a July 4, 1932 gathering at Aurora, Colorado.

7C Fifteen moving brooder house on Purdue Poultry Farm at Purdue University at Lafayette, Indiana on June 4, 1932.

A 7C Fifteen rear seat orchard model working at Inman, South Carolina in 1932.

1D series high Fifteen operating Oliver power lift attachment with three 14-inch listers near South Bend, Indiana in April 1933. The high Fifteen has a 1D serial number, but is really a 7C lifted like a high Ten.

High Fifteen 1D series working with a 9B series #1 Terracer at the August 15, 1932 National Terracing Demonstration at Marysville, Kansas.

Factory photo of the 1D series high-clearance Fifteen.

High Fifteen with factory canopy working in a cane field in the Philippine Islands in 1933.

High Fifteen and #1 Terracer at the National Terracing Demonstration at Marysville, Kansas on August 15, 1932.

More Titles from Iconografix:

*This product is sold under license from Mack Trucks, Inc. Mack is a registered Trademark of Mack Trucks, Inc. All rights reserved.

All Iconografix books are available from direct mail specialty book dealers and bookstores worldwide, or can be ordered from the publisher. For book trade and distribution information or to add your name to our mailing list contact:
Iconografix, PO Box 446, Hudson, Wisconsin, 54016 Telephone: (715) 381-9755, (800) 289-3504 (USA), Fax: (715) 381-9756

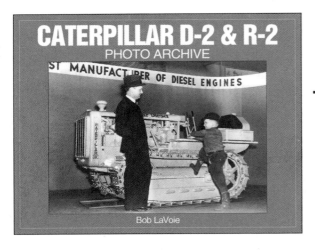

CATERPILLAR D-2 & R-2
PHOTO ARCHIVE
Bob LaVoie

MORE GREAT BOOKS FROM ICONOGRAFIX

CATERPILLAR D-2 & R-2 PHOTO ARCHIVE
ISBN 1-882256-99-9

CATERPILLAR D-8 1933-1974 INCLUDING DIESEL SEVENTY-FIVE & RD-8 PHOTO ARCHIVE
ISBN 1-882256-96-4

CATERPILLAR THIRTY 2ND EDITION INCLUDING BEST THIRTY 6G THIRTY & R-4 PHOTO ARCHIVE
ISBN 1-58388-006-2

CATERPILLAR SIXTY PHOTO ARCHIVE
ISBN 1-882256-05-0

CATERPILLAR POCKET GUIDE THE TRACK-TYPE TRACTORS 1925-1957
ISBN 1-58388-022-4

CATERPILLAR PHOTO GALLERY
ISBN 1-882256-70-0

HOLT TRACTORS PHOTO ARCHIVE
ISBN 1-882256-10-7

CATERPILLAR D-8
1933 - 1974 PHOTO ARCHIVE
Including Diesel Seventy-Five & RD-8
Bob LaVoie

CATERPILLAR THIRTY
PHOTO ARCHIVE 2nd EDITION
Including Best Thirty, 6G Thirty, & R4
Bob LaVoie
Revised 2nd Edition

CATERPILLAR SIXTY
PHOTO ARCHIVE
Edited by P. A. Letourneau

Caterpillar
The Track-type Tractors 1925-1957 Pocket Guide
Bob LaVoie

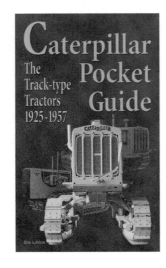

CATERPILLAR
PHOTO GALLERY
Edited by P. A. Letourneau

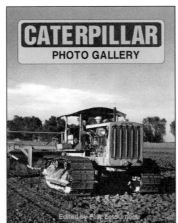

HOLT TRACTORS
PHOTO ARCHIVE
Edited by P. A. Letourneau

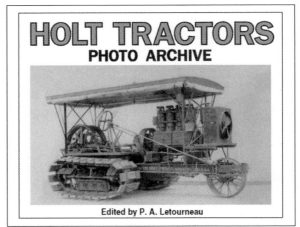